RAYMOND ARROYO

New York Times bestselling author

THE MAGNIFICENT MISCHIEF OF TAD LINCOLN

Illustrated by
JACQUI DAVIS

ZONDERkidz

ZONDERKIDZ

The Magnificent Mischief of Tad Lincoln
Copyright © 2023 by Raymond Arroyo
Illustrations © 2023 by Raymond Arroyo

Requests for information should be addressed to:
Zonderkidz, 3900 Sparks Drive, Grand Rapids, Michigan 49546

Hardcover ISBN 978-0-310-79382-3
Audio download ISBN 978-0-310-79916-0
Ebook ISBN 978-0-310-79915-3

Illustrations: Jacqui Davis
Editor: Katherine Jacobs

Printed in Italy

23 24 25 26 27 28 / RTLO / 21 20 19 18 17 16 15 14 13 12 11 10 9 8 7 6 5 4 3 2 1

As a baby, Thomas Lincoln was called "Tad" by his father, Abe, who thought the boy wriggled and squirmed just like a tadpole.

Tad lived up to his name. He was everywhere at once, creating mischief and mishaps.

Because of his cleft palate, Tad was sometimes difficult to understand. Children would often tease him about his lisp.

So Tad stayed close to his family, playing pranks with his brother Willie—especially on their "paw," Abe, who usually reacted by doubling over in helpless, neighing laughter.

Lincoln was devoted to his boys and would spend evenings reading to them or sharing stories from his own childhood. He once told them how at eight years old, he spied wild turkeys flying over his family's cabin in Indiana. Abe asked to borrow his father's rifle. With his mother's permission, from inside the cabin, he shot through a crack and killed one of the turkeys.

Examining the beautiful dead bird, young Abe regretted what he had done.

"Well, I have never since pulled a trigger on any larger game, boys," Abe told his sons.

"Why not, Paw?" Tad asked.

"My impression is that mercy bears richer fruits than any other attribute."

In 1860, as the clouds of civil war gathered over the nation, Abraham Lincoln was elected president of the United States. Seven-year-old Tad, Willie, and their parents moved to Washington, DC.

But even the White House could not tame Tad's mischievous spirit.

Tad's first order of business was to figure out the mansion's bell system, which summoned the White House workers. Once he found the controls, he rattled every bell in the house —as well as the entire staff.

In Washington, the boys' days were filled with animals. There was a pair of kittens, rabbits, and a pony for riding—both outside and inside.

Tad would often hitch his goat Nanko to an overturned chair and race from room to room inside the White House! If the staff and guests were startled, Mrs. Lincoln took it in stride. "Let the children have a good time," she would say.

But the good times were short-lived. Days after Tad's eighth birthday, war broke out and soldiers from Massachusetts and Rhode Island moved onto the White House grounds to protect the president. Tad and Willie began regularly visiting nearby army encampments with their father.

The experience inspired the Lincoln boys to wear little uniforms at the White House, where they soon built their own fort on the roof. Their favorite game was to make a toy soldier named Jack stand trial. The boys would charge the doll with the crime of deserting his post or falling asleep on duty. They would find him guilty, shoot him with a make-believe cannon, and bury him in the White House flowerbeds.

One day, as Tad, Willie, and their friends were about to give Jack a full military funeral, the White House gardener interrupted their march. To spare his flowerbeds, he encouraged the boys to ask their father "to pardon Jack." Tad leapt at the idea.

"We'll get Paw to fix up a pardon." And he led the charge up to President Lincoln's office. "Paw won't care."

The president's secretary tried to stop the children in the hall. But Mr. Lincoln, hearing the clatter, opened the office door. Right away, Tad begged his father to pardon Jack.

"You know, Tad," the president said, "it's not usual to grant pardons without some sort of hearing. You come in here and tell me why you think Jack should have a pardon."

The boys stormed into the cabinet meeting that was in session and Tad
made his case. After listening patiently, President Lincoln nodded. "It's good
law, Tad, that no man shall twice be put in jeopardy of his life for the same
offense—and you've already shot and buried Jack a dozen times. I guess he's
entitled to a pardon."

Mr. Lincoln scribbled it on a piece of paper and handed it to Tad.

The boy smirked. "I told you he wouldn't care," Tad crowed, exiting the office.

Their playtime and pardons ended when Tad and Willie
were stuck in their beds with fever.

Tad recovered in a few weeks.

But Willie did not.
Overcome by the death of Willie, Mr. Lincoln would
sometimes bolt from meetings and sob privately in the hall.

And without Willie to play with him, Tad wandered the quiet White House all alone. He would often burst into tears at the memory of the fun he and his brother had together.

The loss drew Tad and his father closer than ever before.

Whenever the president gave speeches or ventured out to review the troops, Tad was by his side. And in the White House, he was Mr. Lincoln's shadow.

When relatives of soldiers imprisoned or facing punishment in the battlefield lined up at the White House seeking presidential pardons, Tad would sometimes drag them up to his paw's office. As they pled their case before Mr. Lincoln, Tad would lay on the floor next to the president's desk, listening.

With the war grinding on and the White House still shrouded in grief over the loss of Willie, a gloom hung over the holidays that year.

But when the Lincolns were given a plump, herky-jerky turkey for Christmas, Tad soon made a new friend. Perhaps he even saw something of himself in this odd bird. He named his playmate Jack, just like the toy soldier he and Willie used to play with.

Tad taught Jack to eat from his hand and to trot behind him, and took him out for walks on a leash. Tad didn't care what others thought. He had a playmate again.

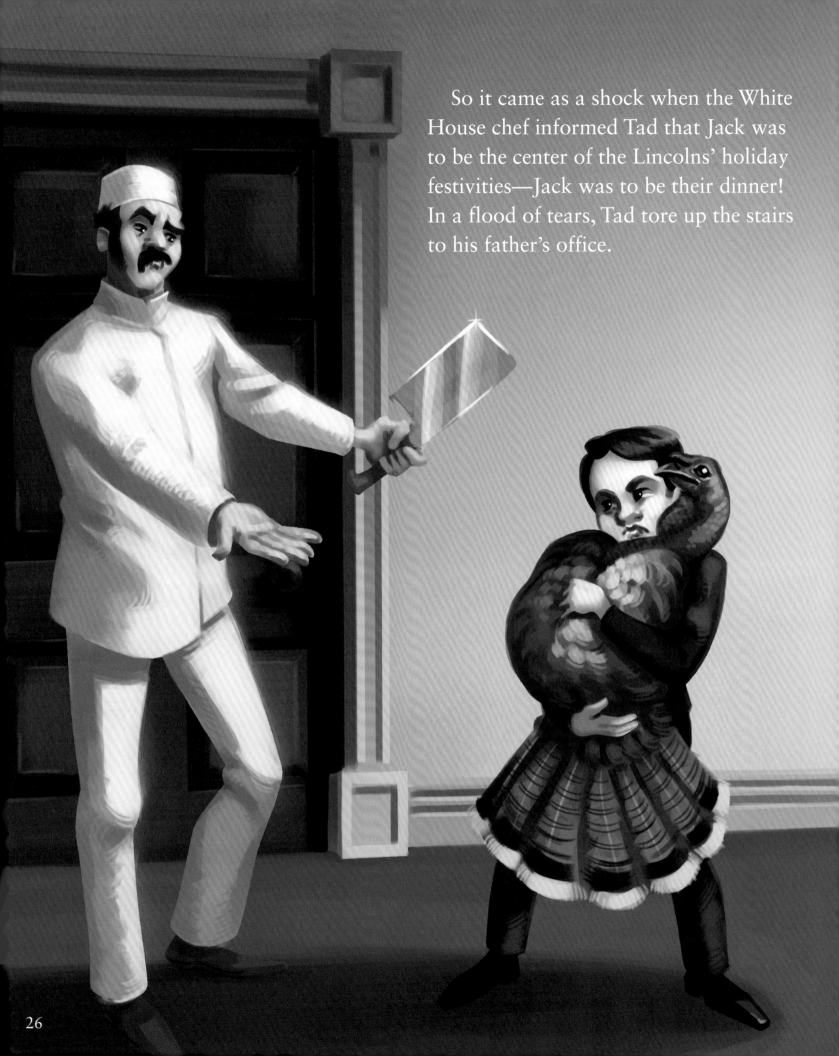

So it came as a shock when the White House chef informed Tad that Jack was to be the center of the Lincolns' holiday festivities—Jack was to be their dinner! In a flood of tears, Tad tore up the stairs to his father's office.

"We can't just forgive these people, Mr. President," a cabinet secretary argued as Tad exploded into the room. "They must pay a severe price for what they've done."

Tad yelled, "Paw! That executioner in the kitchen means to kill Jack! It's wicked. You can't let him."

"Jack was sent to be eaten. I can't help it, son," the president explained. "He's a good turkey. Well-trained too. You can't let him die, Paw," Tad cried, burying his face in Lincoln's coat. "You can't."

The president couldn't help but smile at Tad's sweet pleadings. He reached for his pen and granted Jack the turkey a full reprieve of execution.

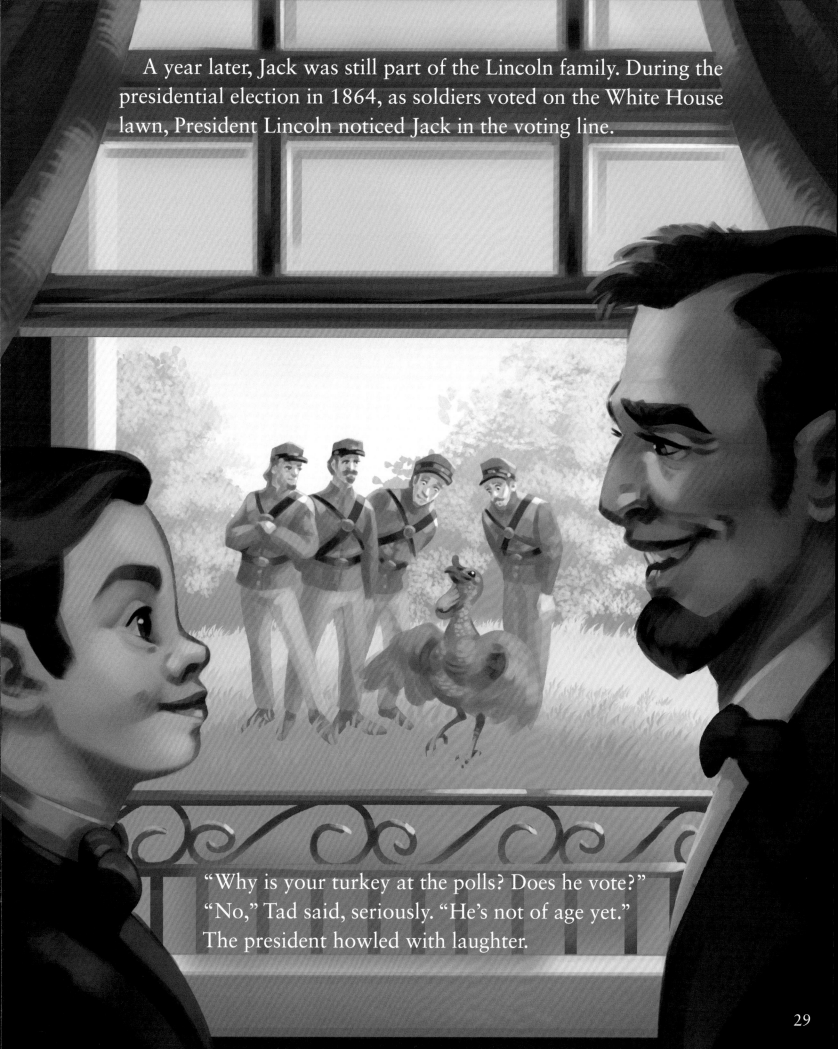

A year later, Jack was still part of the Lincoln family. During the presidential election in 1864, as soldiers voted on the White House lawn, President Lincoln noticed Jack in the voting line.

"Why is your turkey at the polls? Does he vote?"
"No," Tad said, seriously. "He's not of age yet."
The president howled with laughter.

Tad's kind heart and madcap mischief lifted his paw's spirits throughout the darkest days of the Civil War. His constant interruptions reminded the president of the joy beyond war and the need for mercy. Lincoln's acts of forgiveness to bind up a broken country might never have happened if not for his son Tad, urging him to pardon dolls, wayward soldiers, and even a turkey named Jack.

Each year, the president of the United States still pardons a turkey at the White House. It is an ongoing remembrance of Tad Lincoln and his paw, who knew that pardon and mercy heal all wounds, even those of a nation.

Author's Note

Lincoln's cabinet famously hated pardon requests to reach the president personally. He had a soft spot for those in distress—a sensitivity his personal losses only deepened. Lincoln reviewed about 456 civil cases during his presidency. He granted pardons for 375 of them—over 82%. In December of 1863, Lincoln also offered the South full pardons and return of property if they rejoined the union. His generosity and mercy, even amid a bloody war, is a constant theme of his presidency and a huge part of Tad's story.

I was struck during my research by the historic year Tad Lincoln shared with his father in 1863. In January, President Lincoln signed the Emancipation Proclamation, freeing the enslaved people. In November, Lincoln offered his Gettysburg Address—which illness prevented Tad from attending.

As his father reviewed pardons in his office, late into the night, Tad would often fall asleep next to his desk. It was there that Mr. Lincoln established Thanksgiving as a national holiday, in October of 1863. At the time of his presidency, 21 of the 29 states celebrated Thanksgiving, but there was no agreed-upon national date. Lincoln thought it important for the country to share a day of unity. His proclamation declared "the last Thursday of November next as a day of Thanksgiving" to "the Most High God, who, while dealing with us in anger for our sins, hath nevertheless remembered mercy."

Curiously, the tradition of presidential turkey pardons begins with Lincoln, but it would take 100 years for another president to continue it. In 1963, President John F. Kennedy was presented with a turkey wearing a sign reading "Good Eating, Mr. President!" Kennedy felt pity for the bird. "Let's keep him going. It's our Thanksgiving present to him," Kennedy said.

The Nixons and Carters returned their turkeys to nearby farms. But the word "pardon" in reference to a turkey was not formally used until 1987. When President Ronald Reagan received the annual holiday turkey at the White House, he was asked by a reporter if he intended to pardon aides involved in the Iran-Contra affair. Reagan pointed at the 55-pound bird, joking, "I'll pardon him." Every president since has formally pardoned a Thanksgiving turkey. Tad Lincoln's legacy lives on.

Further Reading and Bibliography

Holzer, Harold. *Lincoln As I Knew Him. Gossip, Tributes and Revelations from His Best Friends and Worst Enemies*. Chapel Hill, N.C.: Algonquin Books, 1999.

Reynolds, David S. Abe: *Abraham Lincoln and His Times*. NY: Penguin Press, 2020.

Weaver, John D. *Tad Lincoln, Mischief Maker in the White House*. NY: Dodd, Mead and Company, 1963.

White, Ronald C. *A. Lincoln: A Biography*. NY: Random House, 2009.